The "Perfect" Female,

A Guide Toward Truth, Weight Loss, and Physical Health

Dedicated to my grand-children
Landon, Jaxon and Emma

Many thanks to my beautiful niece Lari Richards, for her support, suggestions, and helpful reviews.

The "Perfect" Female,

A Guide Toward Truth, Weight Loss and Physical Health

Contents

The "Perfect" Female,

A Guide Toward Truth, Weight Loss, and Physical Health

Introduction

Within this volume author, C. R. Tinsley provides an in-depth review of the image of the "perfect" female, as portrayed by the world, and then contrasts that with the image portrayed by God. She also outlines a clear, and easy path towards good physical health.

She shares her own very personal story of carrying a significant amount of unwanted weight, for many years. What caused her weight gain, and how she discovered the truth about the "perfect" female, and, how we should care for our bodies.

Note from the Author: This book is a "must-read" for any female who struggles in any way with weight, self-esteem, or negative body image issues.

Far from being a typical "weight loss" book. Instead, this writing is an honest look at females in our society, and how we can overcome the stereotypes, to find the path to physical health and well-being.

Please do not waste one more moment feeling that you aren't pretty enough, or slim enough. It's time for the truth to be told, and for all women to learn how to truly love themselves, and care for their body.

I pray that each person who discovers this book will find inspiration within these pages. It was extremely difficult for me to put my personal story in print, however, I felt compelled to share my experience, in the faith that it will help others who have struggled with similar issues.

I am absolutely certain that **YOU CAN** take control, and be successful in this journey toward truth, weight loss, and physical health.

May God bless you, and may your physical body reflect the beautiful individual you were created to be.

Where It All Began

I believe the struggle of all Christian women began long ago in the Garden of Eden.

The temptation of Eve was very subtle and particularly cunning. Satan did not disclose his true purpose, but instead, preyed on Eve's mind, to convince her that what God had said, was not "entirely" true and that she wasn't good enough as she was.

Gen.3: 3-5, But from the fruit of the tree which is in the middle of the garden, God has said, 'You shall not eat from it or touch it, or you will die.'" The serpent said to the woman, "You surely will not die!" For God knows that in the day you eat from it, your eyes will be opened, and you will be like God, knowing good and evil."

Try to visualize Satan during the discourse with Eve. I envision him as being kind and compassionate, even expressing concern about Eve's well-being. Ultimately, taking her to the tree of Good-and-Evil, climbing into the tree to prove that he indeed did not die, before offering the secret of how she could be "better". How she could be more than a simple woman. She could be just like God.

This is how it all began. The very point in time where females of every race, and across all decades have been lied to by Satan.

When we look at how God viewed Eve prior to this occurrence, it's clear to see that after he completed the creation process, he declared that **all of his creation was good**.

It's impossible to even consider that what God himself personally created could be anything other than absolutely perfect.

Gen. 1: 26-31, Then God said, "Let Us make man in Our image, according to Our likeness; and let them rule over the fish of the sea and over the birds of the sky and over the cattle and over all the earth, and over every creeping thing that creeps on the earth." God created man in His own image, in the image of God He created him; male and female He created them. God blessed them; and God said to them, "Be fruitful and multiply, and fill the earth, and subdue it; and rule over the fish of the sea and over the birds of the sky and over every living thing that moves on the earth." Then God said, "Behold, I have given you every plant yielding seed that is on the surface of all the earth, and every tree which has fruit yielding seed; it shall be food for you; and to every beast of the earth and to every bird of the sky and to everything that moves on the earth which has life, I have given every green plant for food"; and it was so. God saw all that He had made, and behold, **it was very good**. And there was evening and there was morning, the sixth day.

At that point, Eve was truly the definition of the "perfect" female. There was no other on the entire earth who could begin to compare to her. She was "perfect," pure and innocent; living with the "perfect" male, in their own garden paradise.

I find it interesting that Satan selected Eve as his target. Certainly she was weaker than Adam, however, I feel there was another reason that Eve was targeted. Eve was carrying seeds of the future. She and Adam were to populate the world, however, Eve would be the nurturer and would carry those children inside her womb.

If Satan could cause Eve, the "perfect" female, to feel that she was somehow lacking. Just imagine what lies he could propagate on future generations.

Ultimately, Eve fell prey to Satan's lies, and convinced Adam to do the same. We all know the rest of the story, however, the reason I started at this juncture is that I know that Satan continues to deceive women today, in a similar manner.

His deceptions cause us to feel that we are lacking.

- Not appealing enough

- Not slim enough
- Not dressed well enough

This Was Me

As a teenager, I typically wore medium sized clothes and looking back at pictures now I can easily see that I was an average, young, even pretty girl, however, at the time; I felt very fat and unattractive. Why?

Because society through numerous magazines, and television ads, was presenting an image of the 'perfect" female, that did not look like me. I did not have a super-thin "Barbie-type" body.

1974   1976

That unrealistic image of the "perfect" female, and how I did not resemble that image, caused me to have a very negative opinion of my appearance. Sadly, the result of harboring such thoughts resulted in my body reflecting exactly what I envisioned it to be.

By October of 2013, I was morbidly obese and felt horrible about my body and value as a person. My negative self-image coupled with a poor diet had forged this reality and was holding me hostage.

The Lies

The world perceives the perfect female as someone who fits a "Barbie-type" image. However, if you take a look at the chart below. You can see how misaligned that perception is. The doll clearly does not carry the same proportions as an average female. Yet Satan bombards us daily with similar, unrealistic, and unobtainable images, and presents them as the "perfect" female.

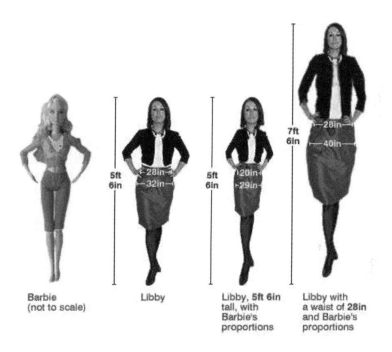

Barbie (not to scale)

Libby

Libby, 5ft 6in tall, with Barbie's proportions

Libby with a waist of 28in and Barbie's proportions

In fact, today's fashion model weighs 23 percent less than the average female. Young women, between the ages of 18 and 34, have only a 7 percent chance of being as slim as a catwalk model, and 1 percent chance of being as thin as a supermodel.

We must also realize that perception, very easily turns into reality for many, just as it did for me.

Let's consider now the ads, and marketing campaigns that we are bombarded with daily, and try to determine their source, and true purpose.

Advertising

Have you ever wondered why women in magazines and, on movie and television screens, look different from the women we encounter on our jobs, in shopping malls, grocery stores, churches, schools, and basically everywhere? It is because altering photographs through air-brushing and photo-shopping is practiced daily in almost all advertising arenas.

Consider this example of a beautiful young lady in the first photo, followed by the actual ad.

The model's size was altered, to create an unrealistically thin figure. The skin tone, and picture tone were altered. Steam was also added, coming from the cup.

Below is another example of an original photo, vs the published version.

The truth is that models, in magazines get enough editing to be nicknamed "Franken Models." Even in films every frame is typically edited. Magazines and ads are simply filled with photographs that have been altered. In many instances this dramatically changes the original photograph.

Advertisers purposely create unrealistically thin bodies, in order to drive product consumption. By creating ideas that are absurdly out of line, with the average female body; they establish, and maintain, a market where their customer base never disappears. This is how Satan maintains control over our thoughts and opinions of our own appearance.

Considering that the diet industry alone generates $33 billion in annual revenue, this strategy has been hugely successful.

Revelation 12:9, And the great dragon was thrown down, the serpent of old who is called the devil and Satan, who deceives the whole world; he was thrown down to the earth, and his angels were thrown down with him.

The Impact On US

Advertisers emphasize sexuality, and the importance of physical attractiveness in their attempts to sell products, but many researchers are becoming concerned that this places undue pressure on women, to focus only on their appearance.

In a recent survey by Teen People magazine, 27 percent of young girls felt that the media pressures them to have a perfect body, and a poll conducted by the international ad agency Saatchi and Saatchi found that ads made women feel unattractive.

Advertising, particularly for women's fashion, style, and cosmetics, clearly has a powerful impact on how most women view themselves, and how they believe they should look.

The average woman sees 400 to 600 advertisements per day, and by the young age of 17, has viewed more than 250,000 commercial messages. Many of those commercials emphasize the huge importance of beauty, particularly those that target women.

One study of Saturday morning toy commercials found that 50% of those commercials were aimed at girls and spoke about physical attractiveness, while none of the commercials aimed at boys referred to appearance.

Other studies found 50 percent of advertisements in teen girl magazines, plus 56 percent of television commercials aimed at female viewers, capitalize on beauty, as the main product appeal.

This constant bombardment of female advertisements causes many young girls to become self-conscious about their bodies, and establishes obsession over their physical appearance, as the primary measure, of their self-worth.

Many health professionals are now concerned by this prevalence of distorted body images among women. Research shows that 75 percent of women who are a "normal" weight, and size, believe themselves to be overweight. In other words, they are believing the lies, instead of the truth.

What is particularly scary is that over 50 percent, of 9 and 10-year-old girls, feel better about themselves if they are on a diet, even though the Center for Disease Control and Prevention, reported that only 18 percent of adolescents are actually overweight.

The result, of these unrealistic images, is countless women, both young and old, who harbor negative views of their own bodies. Even though their body may very well be a normal, average size, and weight.

When this happens, many of those women tend to exhibit unhealthy behavior, as they strive for the ultra-thin body, idealized by the media.

Studies have shown that a third of American women in their teens, and twenties begin smoking cigarettes in order to help control their appetite. Some women enter into unhealthy relationships. All in a futile attempt to feel physically attractive.

In addition to leading to the development of disorders, such as anorexia, and bulimia nervosa, a poor body image may also contribute to depression, anxiety, relationship difficulties, the development of substance abuse, and consequently numerous health problems.

Poor self-esteem frequently contributes to troubled relationships, workplace issues, and any area of life that requires a level of self-confidence.

I fully believe that such views regarding the "perfect" female body originated, and are perpetuated, daily by one source, and that source is **Satan and his lies!**

Satan and his lies!

SATAN'S TARGET: Your Mind

SATAN'S WEAPON: Lies

SATAN'S PURPOSE: To make you
ignorant of God's Will

Don't let anyone fool you. Satan is the master liar, and he is extremely good, at what he does!

Satan's lies cause us to look at our bodies, no matter our size, as **inferior, or lacking**. This can have a very negative impact on many. Impacts that are not always immediately evident.

Eating disorders are prevalent throughout our society. Some severe enough to be life-threatening.

Our challenge is to learn to recognize, and overcome his evil deeds. **We have to break this negative thought process now,** and realize that Satan has silently crept into our minds, to create false expectations.

Satan Lies,

God Speaks Truth

Every female body is meant to be as God Almighty himself designed it and not a reflection of the world and Satan's lies.

Let's take a look at scripture to determine exactly how God defines the "perfect" female, and what he deems to be important.

God's Truth

God does not consider physical beauty as a requirement for the "perfect" female.

He is not impressed by outward appearance, but instead, describes the characteristics of the "perfect" female as follows:

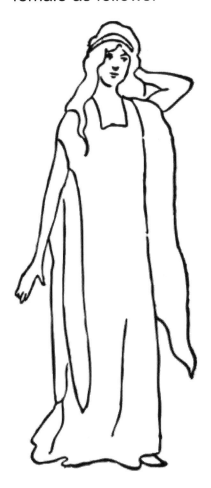

Proverbs 31:10,

- Virtuous

Proverbs 31:30,

- Fearing the LORD

1 Tim. 2:9-10,

- Shamefaced
- Sober
- Good works

1 Tim. 3:11,

- Dignified
- Temperate
- Faithful

1 Peter 3:1-2,

- Chaste

Gen. 1:27, So God created man in his own image, in the image of God he created him; male and female he created them.

Psalm 139:13-14, For you formed my inward parts; you knitted me together in my mother's womb. I praise you, for I am fearfully and wonderfully made. Wonderful are your works; my soul knows it very well.

1 Corinthians 6:19, Do you not know that your bodies are temples of the Holy Spirit, who is in you, whom you have received from God?

Gen. 1:31a, God saw all that he had made, and it was **very good**.

Further instruction tells us:

John 7:24, We are not to judge according to **appearance**.

Luke 16:15, That which is highly esteemed by men, is **detestable** in the sight of God.

Prov. 31:30, Charm is **deceptive**, and beauty is **fleeting**; but a woman who fears the Lord is to be praised.

1 Tim. 2:9-10, Women should **adorn themselves modestly and discreetly**, not with braided hair, gold, pearls, or costly garments, but instead, by good works.

My Journey

By 1993 I had been married for 13 years, and given birth to two beautiful daughters. During that 13-year period, I had slowly gained over 90 pounds.

I prayed each night that I would lose the weight, but, arose morning after morning to a scale, that told me it could not be done.

Satan's lies were causing me to believe that I had no worth, and that my prayers were never going to be answered.

I tried over-the-counter diet pills to no avail, so then, I tried a weight loss solution, where I ate expensive pre-packaged meals, and walked a mile each day.

In just over 12 months I lost 60 pounds, and I thought that I had found the answer, and it was pre-packaged foods, plus exercise.

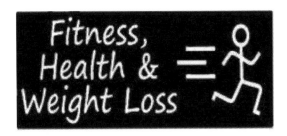

Sadly, for me, that did not provide the long-term solution I was so hoping for.

Once I stopped eating the pre-packaged food, due to the cost, and stopped walking a mile each day; the weight came back and brought more weight with it!

This is true of many who opt for weight-loss surgery, diet pills, or extreme exercise programs. These may provide temporary solutions, but, for many, the weight comes back because the solution they chose could not be maintained long-term

Over the next 10 years I slowly gained more and more weight. I was depressed and felt absolutely helpless. I was trapped inside a body that I had little control over and that I held little regard for.

"Don't step on it . . . it makes you cry."

By 2010 I had been diagnosed with insulin resistance, which meant that my body was overproducing insulin (sugar). My doctor said that this was probably the result of me drinking diet sodas! A "diet" product, causing weight gain. No wonder, I could never lose weight!

According to the doctor diet foods and pre-packaged foods, contain chemicals that your body does not know what to do with. Those chemicals end up being converted into fat. I continued to feel depressed, and helpless.

My doctor suggested I try a diet program offering pre-packaged meals, however, I knew that would only offer a temporary fix. I needed a solution that could be maintained.

The Fundamental Missing Piece

I fully believe that God saw my struggle and in **his timing** brought me to a life-altering experience. An experience that opened my eyes to a fundamental, missing piece. Allow me to share that experience, with you now.

Please think of the most loving moment in your entire life. Focus on the enormous and deep feeling of pure love. Now I ask you to close your eyes for at least 60 seconds and hold onto that feeling. Don't cheat! Before you read further you need to do this. Allow yourself to be completely absorbed into that feeling of absolute love.

As you open your eyes, I want you to understand, that is exactly how GOD LOVES YOU!!!!! Just as you are. No matter what you weight, how old you are, what your education level is, or income bracket you find yourself in, God loves you!

This Humbled Me

It had never occurred to me, that God's love for me was that tremendous, however, that day I fully understood the magnitude of the following truths:

- I AM **HIS** Creation

- I AM made by **HIS** Design

- In **HIS** eyes, I am both **BEAUTIFUL,** and **LOVED**

Because this is absolutely true for each of us we should be **GRATEFUL** for the body he designed and has given to us. Instead of feeling that our body isn't good enough or what "we" want it to be.

You were wonderfully designed. There is only one you. No other person, not even an identical twin, possesses your unique fingerprints.

As with any other truly unique, one-of-kind creation, we are all truly incomparable, in the eyes of God. Our value cannot be comprehended and we cannot be replaced.

We are indeed precious is his sight, therefore, we need to be precious in our own sight as well.

What Came Next?

From that day on, I added love and gratitude for my body into my prayers.

Within a few days I ran into a co-worker who I had not seen in years. He was excited to share with me that he had lost 90 pounds without pre-packaged meals, diet pills, surgery, or even exercise.

I couldn't believe it and had to know how.

He used "**MyFitnessPal.com**".

The www.myfitnesspal.com website offers a free website and smartphone app that tracks diet and exercise to determine optimal caloric intake, and nutrients for a users' goals. It also offers elements intended to motivate users.

For me this tool in conjunction with my new attitude of gratitude and thankfulness to God changed everything.

My Results

October, 2013

December 2017

As of Dec. 30, 2017, I am 24 pounds from my original goal weight and I continue to steadily shed pounds.

My Fitness Pal

Above, I've entered a simple lunch menu, and the tool calculated the calories, carbs, fat, protein, sodium and sugar. In addition, it tracks the totals for the day. This empowers me, and makes it easy to select foods that align with my overall goals.

This tool, when used correctly, will enable you to, not only reach, or maintain your goals, but it will also teach you what food combinations offer a balanced meal plan.

Within the tool, you may also track any exercise you do, and the tool will show you how that impacts your totals for the day.

The tool will track your progress, and notify you if you need to readjust your goals. For example, after dropping a certain amount of weight, you will need to readjust the targets, in order to continue losing at the speed you wish. The tool will then display your adjusted calorie consumption goal.

Before I started using this tool I truly believed that I was making good food choices, however, I quickly found out that I was not. Many of the food choices I was making were just bad.

Another great thing about using "myfitnesspal" is utilizing their free app for smartphones.

When using the smartphone app, you can select the "Nutrition" button at the bottom of the "Diary" page to see charts that will indicate how well your meal plan aligns with your goals, as far as the percentage of carbs, vs, fats, vs. proteins. After selecting "Nutrition", make certain you are on the "Macros" tab.

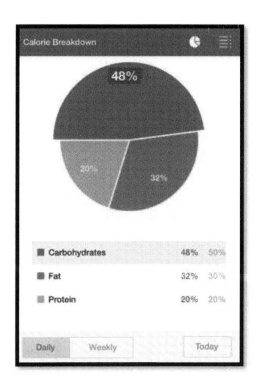

I can't tell you how many times I've added a couple slices of Boar's Head bacon to my meal plan to adjust the protein percentage up, and the carb percentage, down. Having the correct balance is important to maintaining a healthy diet.

Also, once you have completed your food entries on the "Diary" page, you can click on the "Complete" button, and the tool will tell you how much you will weigh in five weeks if you continue a similar meal plan each day. This offers tremendous encouragement to keep you going.

I encourage you to take the time to set up your profile and learn how to use this tool. It is free and very easy to follow. There is absolutely no downside to using it, only positive benefits.

Don't feel that you must deprive your body. If you really want to eat something that is not necessarily good fuel for your body, then eat it. Just get back on your plan afterwards and move forward towards a healthy body and lifestyle.

Before we touch on that, let's take a moment to explore the subject of Gluttony.

Gluttony

Gluttony is generally defined as "excessive eating." The Bible, often mentions gluttony alongside drunkenness and identifies it as a sin, as shown below:

Proverbs 23:21, For the drunkard and the glutton will come to poverty, and slumber will clothe them with rags.

We need to understand that many judgmental people look at "overweight" people and immediately classify them as gluttons. I submit to you that, this is not only unfair, it is typically far from the truth.

Many overweight people are not overeating, but live on diets possibly not eating enough.

The actual problem is that they are consuming foods, and beverages, that are bad for their body.

Much like properly fueling a vehicle we must consume the proper fuels for our bodies in order for them to function at their best.

Let's look further.

Learning what Foods to Eat

No matter what your size may be, I highly recommend watching the documentary "Food Matters" on Amazon Video, so that you can learn to eat healthily.

I have comprised a short list below of what my doctor advised me is good for the body:

- Bread should be Whole Wheat, Whole Grain.
- Buy Natural, and Organic as much as possible.
- **No Sodas.** (They are full of sugar!)
- Real Eggs, Real Cheese, Real Butter.
- NO DIET ANYTHING!!!!!!! (Especially sodas.)
- Try to make lunch your biggest meal of the day.
- Eat light at night.
- Drink lots of water.
- Limit carbs!
- Eat Fresh Foods.

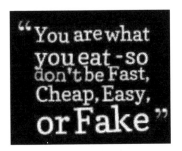

Just Say No To

Fried, Processed, and Sugary Foods!

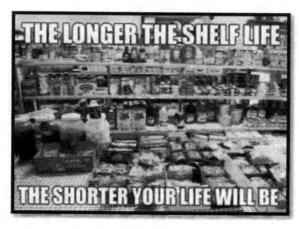

Sugar is Addictive

Scientists have found that sugar is addictive and it stimulates the same pleasure centers of the brain as cocaine or heroin.

Just like hard-core drugs getting off sugar leads to withdrawal and cravings, requiring an actual detox process to break free.

Some experts recommend scaling down your sugar fix over time while others believe that cutting it out altogether is the best way to get through the detox process.

This is harder for some people than others. But please remember that the cravings eventually do go away.

A good way to fight those sugar cravings is by indulging in a small amount of dark chocolate. This will satisfy your craving plus help get through the detox.

Just Say Yes To

~ Top 80 Health Foods ~
Start Eating Healthy Today!

Veggies	Fruits	Grains	Spices
Asparagus	Apples	Barley	Basil
Carrots	Cranberries	Brown Rice	Cilantro
Celery	Blueberries	Buckwheat	Ginger
Kale	Grapefruit	Corn	Oregano
Onions	Oranges	Millet	Parsley
Spinach	Pears	Oats	Peppermint
Squash	Plums	Quinoa	Rosemary
Sweet Potatoes	Rasberries	Rye	Sage
Yams	Watermelon	Spelt	Thyme
Tomatoes	Strawberries	Whole Wheat	Tumeric

Beans	Seafood	Nuts	Drinks
Black Beans	Cod	Almonds	Cranberry Juice
Garbanzo Beans	Halibut	Cashews	Fat Free Milk
Kidney Beans	Mackerel	Flaxseed	Fruit Smoothie
Lima Beans	Oysters	Macadamia Nuts	Green Tea
Miso	Salmons	Peanuts	Mint Tea
Pinto Beans	Sardines	Pistachios	Orange Juice
Navy Beans	Scallops	Pumpkin Seeds	Soy Milk
Soy Beans	Shrimp	Sunflower Seeds	Tomato Juice
Tofu	Talapia	Sesame Seeds	Vegetable Juice
Tempeh	Tuna	Walnuts	Water

  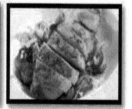

Don't be afraid to eat fresh fruit. The carbs and sugars are natural. Your bodies know how to process them, unlike so many of the carbs that come in pre-packaged, and processed foods.

So much of the food consumed in a typical American diet contains chemicals that the body does not recognize. Guess what happens to those chemicals? Your body converts them into sugar because it doesn't know what else to do with them.

This is why you need to remove "fake" foods from your meal plan. If you like butter buy real butter. If you want cheese, go for real cheese and not a product that comes wrapped in plastic or in a tube.

Do **NOT** eat any product that includes the name "diet" in the title. Stop using artificial sweeteners. Instead, use something natural such as honey.

Making the Change

Understand this; you are **good enough!** However, if you want to change, you have to be prepared to do things differently and be committed to fueling your body with healthy, nutritious meals. Not because you want to look like a fashion model, but because you want to care for the amazingly beautiful, wonder-filled body, that our God blessed you with.

Consider the suggestions below:

Breakfast - Start your day off with a healthy breakfast.

Drink Water - Drinking plenty of water before meals will reduce the opportunity to overfill the stomach with calorie dense foods.

Use Smaller Plates – Using small plates helps reduce not only food amount but can trigger feelings of fullness with lesser amounts.

Mindful Eating – Enjoy and appreciate how the food smells, looks, tastes, etc.

Rethink Seconds – It takes the mind and stomach time to connect and trigger a complete "I'm full" response. Instead of scarfing down your meal quickly, slow down and really enjoy what you're eating.

There are also studies that have shown that specific diets can reverse the effects of illnesses such as heart disease, cancer, and diabetes. If you are interested in getting more information on this subject, I refer you to a book titled "The China Study" by T. Colin Campbell, PhD and Thomas M. Campbell II, MD. Their book promotes an entirely plant-based diet. No meats or products made from animal sources such as eggs, milk, or dairy. It is not necessary to follow a plant-based diet if your objective is to lose weight, however, if you are also struggling with health issues, you may want to consider that approach for better health.

I personally severely limit any consumption of red meat but do enjoy fish, organically-raised chicken breasts, and organically-raised turkey breast.

I understand that for many, all of this represents a significant change in diet, it certainly did for me, however, once your body becomes accustomed to healthy your body will soon begin to crave healthy foods., but Your body will soon begin to crave healthy foods.

Remember it's ok to splurge every now and then and eat something that doesn't conform to your new plan. Just get back on your plan the following day, and move forward with absolute confidence that, you **can do this**.

You will find encouragement when you begin seeing the difference in your appearance and in the way you feel.

Note: Do not step on the scales every day. The female body is made up of 45 to 60 percent water so weight can, and will, fluctuate. Sometimes by a few pounds each day.

The best practice is to establish one day of the week as your "weigh-in" day. Also, it's best to weigh in at the same time of day wearing no clothing, or similar weight clothing each time. This will provide you with the most accurate assessment of your progress as you go through this journey towards better physical health.

The saying below is true:

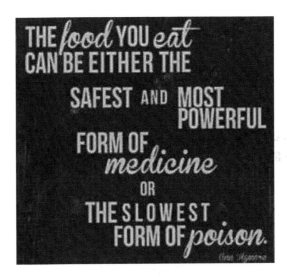

Please consider that statement for a moment before moving forward. The decision is completely up to you. After carrying excess weight for half of my life, I am here as a testament to you that **YOU CAN DO THIS!** If I can; anyone can. Please do not allow Satan's lies, to creep into your subconscious, and create doubt, and fear.

Understand that only **YOU** can change your life. No one can do it for you. You have nothing to lose and much to gain by taking this journey.

Supporting Each Other

One of the key factors in being successful at changing our lives and improving our physical health is support from others and supporting others ourselves.

Eccl. 4:9-10, Two are better than one, because they have a good return for their labor: If either of them falls down, one can help the other up. But pity anyone who falls and has no one to help them up.

The answer for that is a loving, supportive spouse, however, a Christian Sister, or close friend, may also fill this role. We should help each other on this journey.

1 Thess. 5:11, Therefore encourage one another and build one another up, just as you are doing.

I fully believe that by joining together, to fight the lies, we can change the future. We can overcome Satan's grip on us.

Psychological research has found that a group approach helps, at least in the short-term. Most people find it easier to stick with any "weight-loss" plan where you have the support of others. It's great to be able to share meal plans and new recipes to support a healthy diet with others.

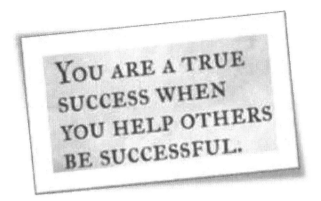

YOU ARE A TRUE SUCCESS WHEN YOU HELP OTHERS BE SUCCESSFUL.

I find myself excitedly sharing some of the new creations that come out of my kitchen. I am constantly using my crock pot to make fresh vegetable soups. I've found that I love to bake whole-grain bread, and experiment with different spices and ingredients. The last time I prepared spaghetti I used whole-grain pasta, Newman's tomato and basil sauce, and ground turkey as my meat. I added various Italian seasonings and it was the best spaghetti I have ever put in my mouth. I had to stop my husband from getting a 3rd helping of it.

Sharing and supporting in this manner can make the difference between success and failure.

I fully believe that by joining together, to fight the lies, we can change the future. We can overcome Satan's grip on females within our society, and allow women to truly appreciate their bodies, and carry a renewed respect for their true value.

Our Thoughts Matter

God created this entire universe and everything within it, not with hammer and nails, but with the enormous power of his mind. Christ healed many people while here on this earth with only the power of his mind.

Consider the absolute fact that we are created in their image. Therefore, it makes sense that our minds work in a very similar manner. This means that our thoughts carry greater power than most realize.

Have you ever wondered why Jesus taught that if anyone looks at a woman to lust after her has already committed adultery?

Matt. 5:27-28, You have heard that it was said, 'Do not commit adultery.' But I tell you that anyone who looks at a woman to lust after her has already committed adultery with her in his heart.

1 John 3:15, Everyone who hates his brother is a murderer, and you know that eternal life does not reside in a murderer.

Our thoughts project outwardly, and create a field of either love, appreciation, negativity, or hate.

A book I read recently suggest this outward "field of thought", is a "prayer field", and each of those "prayers", are heard by God. Therefore, we must make a conscious effort to travel through this life with thoughts of love, appreciation, and compassion.

Think of how God must feel if we do not love, and care for the beautiful body he designed just for us.

I know, from personal experience that I enjoy giving gifts to those who appreciate the gift, however, gifts given to those who do not appreciate them, cause me to rethink giving more.

Consider this. If you spend a great deal of time and effort selecting just the right gift for a child, and that child responds with something to the effect of "why did you give me that? That's not what I wanted." Does it create within you a desire to give them more gifts? No it does not.

I submit to you that our God feels much the same way when we do not appreciate the gift of the physical body he blessed each of us with. Why should he desire to give us more?

I believe this may be part of the reason behind my weight gain. Since my thoughts were constantly telling God that the body he gave me, even in size 12 and 14 clothing, was hugely fat and unattractive; that he allowed my body to reflect the image that I held within my heart and mind of myself.

I believe as well that he intended to use me and my experience, to help others see the truth of their beauty and the wonderfully designed bodies that God has given us.

The most beautiful art in this entire world is art that was created by God himself. Just like the sunset captured in the photograph below; you are a beautiful and unique piece of art created by the master artist.

We are Commanded to Love

When we look through eyes of love at our own body, we see things very differently.

How many of you have held a newborn baby? We know that it doesn't matter if the baby is shriveled like a prune, or covered with amniotic fluid; it is absolutely **beautiful and precious.** Especially in the eyes of the parent.

We need to understand that is how God sees us.

No matter our size; skin color; age; physical attributes; or appearance. He looks at us through **parental eyes of absolute love**.

Those of you who have children know that there are many times when the child wants to do things that will bring pleasure or make them happy, instead of doing what is best for them.

I give you the example of ta st grader who is asked: "what would you like to do today at school?" The response will typically be to have recess all day, however, as parents we understand that the most important part of school is not recess.

We show love for the child through teaching them discipline. We don't let them stay in recess all day but instead, make certain that the majority of their school time is spent in classes where they study reading, writing, and arithmetic.

We have to learn to treat ourselves in this same manner. We cannot eat only those foods that bring pleasure and taste good, such as fried foods, sweet foods, or drinks loaded with sugar. We must out of love for ourselves, learn to properly feed our bodies so that we can remain strong and healthy. One of my favorite desserts of all time is key-lime pie, however, I understand that as a source of fuel for my body, that is a poor choice.

The China study that I mentioned earlier suggests that diseases such as diabetes, cancer, and hypertension are sometimes genetic, however, approximately 90% of those diseases can be traced to poor diet as the primary causative factor.

What Does It All Mean?

We should **never** strive to resemble an image created by the world but **should** care for our bodies, as a precious gift from our Father.

Caring for, and treasuring our bodies, will help us **grow closer to God**. However, we need to all understand that not every female body was designed to be a size 6. God made each one of us **different, totally unique.**

It's imperative that we understand this and that we raise our children to know how very much God loves them, just as they are. We must shield and protect them from Satan's lies, and teach them to care for their body as a treasured gift from God.

We also need to understand that God created each of us by a unique pattern. A pattern that was designed with intent and purpose. Can you imagine how dull this world would be if we all looked alike, were the same physical size and weight? What if we were all the same race or gender?

If we look at God's creation in the animal kingdom you will see that there are many, many different animals with different sizes, different colors, different abilities, and different purposes or talents. The flowers in our gardens are not 100% alike, even when you are looking at the same type of bloom. Some may be short while some are long. Some may reflect a beautiful shade of red, while others may be yellow, blue, or even multi-colored.

Each possesses its own unique style and appearance. all based on God's design. I personally am 5' 1" tall and do not expect to have the same weight or size as a person who is 5' 7" tall. Nor should I.

One thing I noticed while painting with friends was tha each of the paintings, even though we all had the same type of canvas, same amount, and color of paint, the same type of paint brushes; each painting was completely unique, and carried its own beauty. Much as each person is unique and carries their own personal beauty.

I read a post on Facebook recently that went something like this: There once was a crow who lived in the woods. He was happy with his life and never wanted for anything. But one day the crow saw a dove and thought, that dove is so bright and beautiful. By comparison, I am so dark and dull.

The crow approached the dove and said, "you are so beautiful, you must be the happiest bird alive." The dove replied that he used to think that he was the happiest bird alive until he saw a robin with a vibrant red chest. He felt plain by comparison and said that the robin must be the happiest bird alive.

The crow then visited the robin and told him, "you are so beautiful, you must be the happiest bird alive." The robin responded that he once thought that he was the happiest bird alive, but then one day he saw a peacock and was impressed by his vibrant coloring. He went on to say that his red chest was boring by comparison, therefore, he felt that the peacock must be the happiest bird alive.

The crow then flew to a zoo to meet the peacock. Many people were flocking around taking pictures of the beautiful bird. When the crowd left, the crow said to the peacock, "you are so beautiful, you must be the happiest bird alive." The peacock responded, "I thought I was the happiest bird alive, but then they put me in a cage because of my beauty. Sometimes I look at the sky and see crows flying free, and all I want is to be a crow. I think the crow must be the happiest bird alive."

By comparing ourselves to others we can lose sight of our own blessings. The secret to true happiness is to be grateful to God, for what we have, and not upset over what we think we lack.

Physical Activity – Exercise

I would be remiss if I failed to mention the importance of physical activity.

My doctor explained to me that diet is the most critical factor in any weight-loss regiment, and not exercise. Because of this, I do not believe that you have to work out at a gym each day or do extreme exercises. In truth, I caution against any exercise routine, or lifestyle change, that cannot be maintained long-term.

Being a "couch potato" is unhealthy, and can result in muscle loss, and lead to a host of other issues. I believe the solution is to have a routine of, physical activity, that can be maintained long-term. Think ahead. If you decide to run 5-miles a day in order to lose weight, what is going to happen when you are no longer able to continue that activity?

A sensible and maintainable routine is the best approach, even if is only yoga, walking, or stretches, for 30 minutes each day. This will keep your muscles strong and offer numerous health benefits.

According to a recent study by the Mayo Clinic, the health benefits listed below can be derived from 30-minutes of daily exercise:

- **Lower blood pressure**: A reduction of 5 to 10 millimeters of mercury (mm Hg) is possible. In some cases, that's enough to prevent or reduce the need for blood pressure medications.

- **Improve cholesterol**: Exercise often increases the concentration of high-density lipoprotein (HDL or "good" cholesterol in the blood), especially when accompanied by weight loss. Exercise also helps reduce triglyceride levels.

- **Prevent or manage type 2 diabetes**: Exercise helps insulin work better, lowering blood sugar.

- **Manage weight**: Coupling exercise with a healthy diet is the best way to shed fat and maintain a healthier body composition.

- **Prevent osteoporosis**: Exercise may increase bone density and protect against bone mass decline, especially if weight-bearing activities are involved.

- **Prevent cancer**: Exercise has been shown to strengthen the immune system, improve circulation, reduce body fat and speed digestion. Each has a role in preventing cancer, particularly cancers of the colon, prostate, uterine lining, and breast.

- **Maintain mental well-being**: Exercise may help reduce stress, improve mild-to-moderate depression and anxiety, improve sleep and boost moods.

- **Increase energy and stamina**: A lack of energy often results from inactivity, not age.

Try to find something that you enjoy. If you enjoy walking through a garden. Find a local park or a quiet place where you can walk each day.

If you enjoy gym memberships where you are able to use various different forms of equipment then, by all means, join a local gym. Just please do not establish a pattern that will be too difficult, or strenuous to follow as you age.

I personally enjoy stretching and doing yoga positions while listening to soft, soothing music. For me, that provides time to not only exercise my muscles, but also meditate, and commune with God.

Parting Messages

We **don't** need to be a certain size, or weight, to please God, or to be proud of our own bodies, however, if any person wants to change their appearance, and improve their physical health; then a change in diet, and lifestyle is required.

We all need to truly appreciate, and offer gratitude to God, for our bodies and the nourishment he provides to sustain those bodies.

I pray each day that the Lord will bless the food I eat, and help me to select foods that will nourish, and fortify my body; flushing out all diseased cells and unneeded fat cells.

As we wrap up, I ask that you consider this final verse:

1 Cor.10:31, So, whether you eat or drink, or whatever you do, do all to the glory of God.

May God go with you on this journey. Feel free to use the following pages to capture any notes, cooking tips, new recipes, or contact information for any Christian Sister, or friend that you may be supporting on this journey.

_____

_____

_____

_____

_____

_____

_____

_____

_____

_____

_____

_____

_____

_____

_____

_____

_____

_____

_____

_____

Follow author C.R. Tinsley online at:
https://www.facebook.com/authorcrtinsley/
https://authorcrtinsley.wixsite.com/mysite

80218611R00053

Made in the USA
Lexington, KY
31 January 2018